TOP SECRET! Codes to Crack

BURTON
ALBERT, Jr.

Illustrated by
Jerry
Warshaw

Albert Whitman & Company, Niles, Illinois

With love for Lois, who shares my secrets

Library of Congress Cataloging-in-Publication Data

Albert, Burton.
  Top secret!

  Summary: An illustrated explanation of twenty-eight
secret codes that can be used to send messages.
  1. Ciphers—Juvenile literature. [1. Ciphers]
I. Warshaw, Jerry, ill. II. Title
Z103.3.A537   1987   652'.8   87-2146
ISBN 0-8075-8027-9 (lib. bdg.)

The text of this book is set in twelve-point Helios.

Text ©1987 by Burton Albert, Jr.
Illustrations ©1987 by Albert Whitman & Company
Published in 1987 by Albert Whitman & Company,
Niles, Illinois
Published simultaneously in Canada by
General Publishing, Limited, Toronto
All rights reserved. Printed in U.S.A.
10 9 8 7 6 5 4 3 2 1

QUICK! Scurry to your tented blanket or treehouse. . .along with this book. And don't let ANYONE — except your very closest-forever clubmates — know that you've discovered this treasure trove of code keys.

Like magic, they will show you how to write hidden messages and to crack the more than 115 brainbusters on the pages that follow. (Shhh. . .the Answer File is on page 30.)

Now. . .is your flashlight in working order? Are the batteries fresh? If so, get ready to beam your way to:

Riddles, Daffynitions, and Puzzles of All Sorts

Have fun with. . .

Oodles of Doodles, Balloon-o-Grams, Recipes, Autographs and Clockfaces, Bookstacks, Script Letters, and Punctuation Marks

. . .as well as:

Coded Flags, Calendars and Telescopes, License Plates, Bumper Stumpers, and more!

Spy those picture hints on how to send mystery messages using:

Colored Pens and Markers   **Greeting Cards**
Magazine Cut-Outs   **Bookmarks**
Stamps and Sticker Labels

And NEVER, EVER forget. You're one of the KIDS: **K**EEPERS OF **I**RONCLAD **D**ARK **S**ECRETS. And to make your messages stay Tip-Top Hush-Hush, leave no mark in this book. Baffle and addle the wits of others. For yourself, have a carnival of fun.

PSSSST: If you like what you find here, then be sure to prowl about for the other titles in this series: **Codes for Kids, More Codes for Kids**, and **Code Busters!** You'll be surprised and delighted by the secrets they hold!

DOTS 'N BLOTS

Spot the dot or blot. If it falls on a letter, the letter forms a part of a word in the TSM, the Top-Secret Message. Each green letter in the message signals the end of a word. Dots and blots that simply splotch the paper are **misleads**. A mislead is a letter, word, or other mark that makes a message look like scribble-scrabble.

TRY THE KEY: CRACK THE CODES

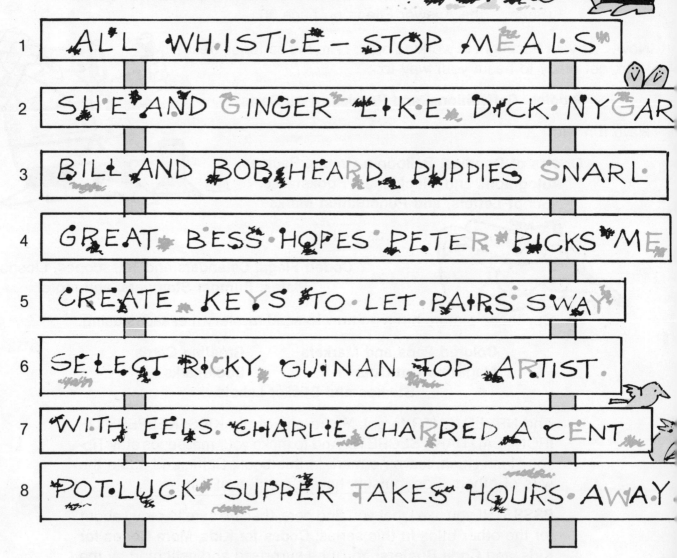

1. ALL WHISTLE – STOP MEALS
2. SHE AND GINGER LIKE DICK NYGAR
3. BILL AND BOB HEARD PUPPIES SNARL
4. GREAT BESS HOPES PETER PICKS ME
5. CREATE KEYS TO LET PAIRS SWAY
6. SELECT RICKY GUINAN TOP ARTIST
7. WITH EELS CHARLIE CHARRED A CENT
8. POT·LUCK SUPPER TAKES HOURS AWAY

Are you a topnotch dot 'n blot splotter? Trot to the Answer File on page 30 and see.

TELESCOPES

Telescope a wish...a dream...by sliding your eyes topside of a line. When you spy a mark that looks like one of these...

...peek at the letter below the mark. It is part of the coded message. Other letters as well as the marks below the line defy the pirating pries of Codebuster McSly. Breaks in a line separate one word from another.

TRY THE KEY: CRACK THE CODES

1
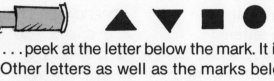

▲B●∪OG■OAT■⊙	B▲▲∇D	JOE■■T	DO⊙OA▲SOK
C●ATSIT■LIES	KILNS	⊙T∇HEW	HAS■KEY▲

2

WE▲●⊙A■K■Y∇	K■ITT⊙EN	∇BOOK■■A●⊙
A●QU■■ETEPN	▲OLD∇F●Z	H■EADRATES

3

L∇●●■●OOKS	G■▲HO∇⊙L∇∇∇	HOL∇P■OT■●YO■
UPRAINNTIE	KYOFURSHELF	AREALINGBOLWS

BRANDING IRONS

Western folk love roundin' up herds of coded letters that look like marks from branding irons. The hush-hush letters are either circled or hooked together in some kind of cowpokin' fashion. Uncircled letters keep rustlers off the trail, as do the different designs, colors, and sizes. A dot under a letter signals the end of a word.

TRY THE KEY: CRACK THE CODES

1 IF LO ᵁAṬE THE©ATE®R AⅎTE®R

2 LA®S P©NED ⊙FⅎE®R T⊙ HEA̤R EA̤CH

3 ⅈPTE AND RUⅎ⑤

FIZZLER CURLS

Turn a snooper's steam to fizzle drizzle.

1. Print the first part of a sentence **backward** in uppercase letters. Spread them out and drop a dot under each letter that ends a word:

UPPERCASE LETTERS
A B C D E F G H I
J K L M N O P Q
R S T U V W X Y Z

WATCH FOR = ṚO F ḤC TA W

2. With lowercase letters, insert the rest of the message in between the uppercase letters. Begin at the right, glide left, and freckle the ending letters with dots as well.

LOWERCASE LETTERS
a b c d e f g h i
j k l m n o p q
r s t u v w x y z

THE CABOOSE = es ṚOooFbaḤCceTAhwt

If you wish, print your messages on paper-strip curl-ups and color some letters and dots to keep code trackers pluggin' and chuggin'.

TRY THE KEY: CRACK THE CODES

HINT: In the messages below, this I is uppercase; this $|$ is the lowercase letter that comes between k and m.

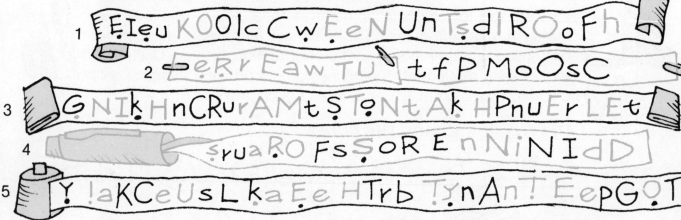

1. ḞIịeụKOOlcCẉEeNUnṬṣdIROoFh
2. ṢeṚᵣEawTU tfPMoOsC
3. GNIḳHnCRᵤᵣAMtṢTọNtAḳHPnụErLEt
4. ṣᵣuaṚOFsṢOREnNiNIdD
5. Ỵ!aKCeUsLḳaḞ.eHTrbṬᵧnAṬEepGQ̣T

Remember Operation DUD: **D**erail **U**nsuspecting **D**ecoders. Keep all pages clean so no markings by pen or pencil will show what the messages mean.

To unfurl a message in this code, eye the lines and creases. If a line points to a letter or if a crease runs through a letter, the letter is part of the secret word. Other marks, numerals, and letters lead sleuths to parade a different route.

TRY THE KEY: CRACK THE CODES

1 **What did the light bulb keep asking?**

2 **Whenever the parakeets sang so high, what did the canary sing?**

3 **What did the Chinese emperor order the lumberjack to do?**

4 **What did the lawyer look for in the ocean?**

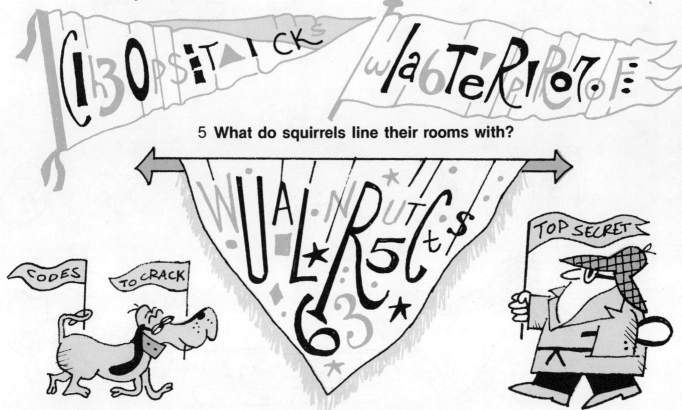

5 **What do squirrels line their rooms with?**

SPAGHETTI LETTERS

Dish up a mishmash of noodle doodles. Write your message **backward** in script — with letters on their sides:

GEMS =

Then add oodles of noodles as miscues:

THE ALPHABET IN SCRIPT

a A b B c C d D e E
f F g G h H i I
j J k K l L m M n N
o O p P q Q r R s S
t T u U v V w W x X
y Y z Z

TRY THE KEY: CRACK THE CODES

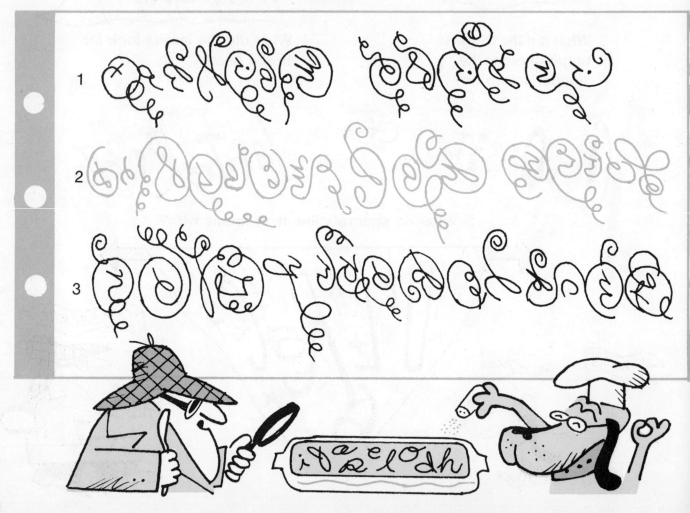

1

2

3

VOWEL SHAPES

To sniggle the snouts of sneak-abouts, use shapes like these in place of vowels:

A E I O U (with shapes: triangle, flag, small square, circle, square)

Picture the message you want to hide:

BUCKSKIN   JACKET

Then, starting from the right, print each word **backward**. Substitute the shape for the vowel the shape is replacing. And, if you wish, use different sizes and colors to fog the coded path.

BUCKSKIN   JACKET

N I k S k c ■ b   T E K C ▲ j

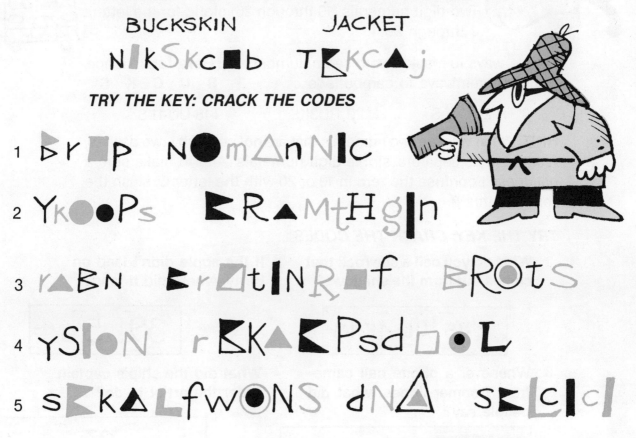

TRY THE KEY: CRACK THE CODES

1. ▷ r ■ p   N ● m △ n N I c

2. Y k ● ● P s   E R ▲ M t H g I n

3. r ▲ B N   E r ▫ t I N R ◾ f   B R ● t s

4. Y S I ● N   r E K ▲ E P s d ▢ ● L

5. s E K ▲ L f w ● N S   d N △   s E L c I c

9

Sometimes, codes are based on the positions of the letters of the alphabet. In this baffler, letters may stand for themselves **or** be cued by a numeral in this A-to-Z Key:

POSITION:	1	2	3	4	5	6	7	8	9	10	11	12	13	14	15	16	17	18	19	20	21	22	23	24	25	26
LETTER:	A	B	C	D	E	F	G	H	I	J	K	L	M	N	O	P	Q	R	S	T	U	V	W	X	Y	Z

Every letter that's shown is part of the hidden message.

Single-digit numerals (1 through 9) stand for the letters A through I, as signaled by the key.

Two-digit numerals (10 through 26) stand for the letters J through Z.

Hence, ways to mask a word seem numberless. Here, for instance, are just three ways to camouflage... **T R U C K S**

■ TR-21-C-11-S ■ 2Ø-RU3KS ■ T-18-UC-11-S

HINT: When you see two numerals that are **not** set off by two dashes, read them as separate, single-digit numerals. And to make sure a pal doesn't confuse the zero in 10 or 20 with the letter O, slash the zero like this Ø.

TRY THE KEY: CRACK THE CODES

1 What do you call a shy rock that comes out from the shadows?

2-15-UL-4E-18-

2 If the apple didn't land on Betty, where did it land?

39 D5-18-

3 Whenever a phone call came from Boomer Jones, what did people say?

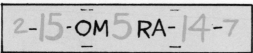
2-15-OM5RA-14-7

4 What did the ship's captain order the artist to do?

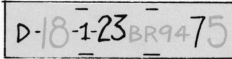
D-18-1-23 BR94 75

5 What do you call a Halloween hag that lives on the beach?

-19 A-14-D-23-9C-8

6 Which insects ride the hides of fire-spewing monsters?

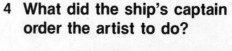
4-18-A7-15-N6-12-9E-19-

CODE-A-CARDS AND BOOKMARKS

Design your own cards and "marks." Just clip, code, and color. In coding, keep in mind how you can write messages using the A-to-Z Key. But instead of letting dashes signal two-digit numerals, show these numerals in color. Let single-digit numerals remain black:

B E N   L O V E S   M I N D Y
2 E 14   12 O V 5 19   13 9 14 D 25

Sometimes you may also want to link four numerals together to represent two sets of two-digit numerals. When you do that, write all four numerals in the same color:

M Y   P U P
13 25   P 21 16

TRY THE KEY: CRACK THE CODES

1. D15N'20
   2LO23
   I20
   514J15Y!

2. 19 I7 14 21 P
   6 O 18
   1325 16A18T25

YES

3. SHIP AHOY!
   23A22E19
   06
   715154B255

4. P1512A18
   TO: 251R
   FROM:
   G18A25
   S17219R18EL.

5. BOOKMARK
   112L'19
   23512L
   2081T
   5449
   W51212

11

BUBBLE DOUBLES

All uppercase letters are part of a secret message, except the bubble doubles that look like this:

They contain lowercase letters. And in a bubble double, only the lowercase letter is read:

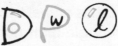 = **owl**

A question mark (**?**) or exclamation point (**!**) signals the end of a word. Colors and empty bubbles are miscues. So, too, is a lowercase letter standing by itself:

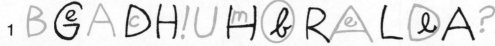 = **OWL IN TREE**

TRY THE KEY: CRACK THE CODES

1 B⓮A DH!UH⓫RALⓛA?

2 a⓲?AR!OⓖⓔR?YAmUU!mBⓣRⓠE?

3 b⓪ⓒlⓖD!YBⓟU?ⓣRⓐfD⓮!
   ⓣHⓒmAT?ⓔ ⓒhOsIH⓷zy?

4 zaPU⓰ⓓeH?¡TQE!⓾ogⓌⓎ?
   BⓙⓤⓢTAgaN?

5 M⓮S⓰ⓢAdGⓎ?hⓛttⓗ!KOP?
   FOWEⓡⓎ?ⓔⓓⓘSiCe!

12

Seven lowercase letters have ascenders, or "stick-up" parts, that extend above the body of the letter. The seven are:

	PRINT	SCRIPT
ASCENDER BODY	b d f h k l t	b d f h k l t

Use these stick-up parts to signal letters in a coded message showing a pair of autographs.

Tuck your message in the top autograph. In the bottom autograph, plant lowercase letters with stick-ups to point out the secret meaning.

Nicolet Ettery

Kathleen Allonther = **NICE TRY**

TRY THE KEY: CRACK THE CODES

1 *Anthony T. Timpkins*
  Ellen-Edith Adams

2 *Penelope C. Thornwood*
  Edward Blake Bellheim

3 *HARVEY DILLON KINGMAN*
  Rachel Jill Baffa

FRAC FLACK

Q: What's the **sum** of the numerals in each fraction? (For example, picture 1/5 as 1 + 5 = 6; 4/7 as 4 + 7 = 11; and so on.)

Q: What letter in this **Reverse** Z-to-A Key does the **sum** match?

POSITION:	1	2	3	4	5	6	7	8	9	10	11	12	13	14	15	16	17	18	19	20	21	22	23	24	25	26
LETTER:	Z	Y	X	W	V	U	T	S	R	Q	P	O	N	M	L	K	J	I	H	G	F	E	D	C	B	A

Answer those two questions, and you can crack frac flack like that swapped between Todd and Bob below.

HINT: When you see [1/2 + 1/2], think of it as **1**, standing for the letter **Z** in the key.

TRY THE KEY: CRACK THE CODES

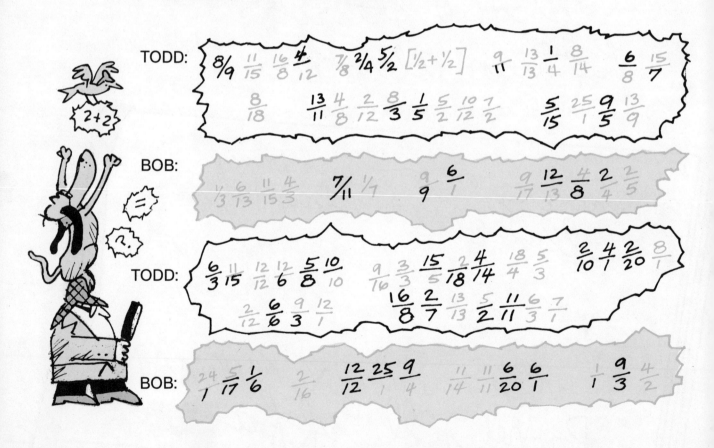

X AND THE LETTER TWINS

The "cancellation mark" across each sticker stamp veils a secret message. To figure it out, look for each **X** and set of letter twins, such as **aa**, **Bb**, **CC**, and so on. The letter that follows the X or twin helps uncover the sticker stumper.

TRY THE KEY: CRACK THE CODES

1

XseeTXABbY
XTXHffexRgge

2

FfSXHXidDPXYooAXRXd

3

XwhHeXaLLR
ccYXoXugGr
SsmXAHhsXK

PUZZLE BOUNCE

In the crossword puzzle, read the word marked **1**. Follow that word with the word or phrase given as **Clue 1**. Then read the second word in the puzzle and follow it with the clue marked **2**. Bounce back and forth like this to get the beat on the hidden meaning.

TRY THE KEY: CRACK THE CODES

1

¹D	O	²P	L	A	N
	³T	H	E	⁴B	I G
⁵C	O	N	T	E	S T

Clues

1 You
2 To enter
3 Town's
4 Leapfrog

2

¹B	E	²B	R	I	N	G
³N	E	W	⁴A	L	O	N G
	⁵M	I	G	H	T	⁶O N
⁷D	I	V	E		⁸O	F
	⁹F	R	I	E	N	D S

Clues

1 Sure to   5 Go
2 Your   6 A scuba
3 Goggles   7 With all
4 We   8 Nick's

15

BALLOON·O·GRAMS

As your eyes glide left to right, top to bottom, figure out the **sum** of the symbols shown in each part of the balloon's grid:

● = 1   ■ = 2   ⋁ = 5   ✕ = 10   ⊙ = 20

Then, using the A-to-Z Key below, target the letter that matches the sum. Find the name of the city the balloon comes from.

POSITION: 1 2 3 4 5 6 7 8 9 10 11 12 13 14 15 16 17 18 19 20 21 22 23 24 25 26

LETTER: A B C D E F G H I J K L M N O P Q R S T U V W X Y Z

TRY THE KEY: CRACK THE CODES

HINT: Ignore empty grids. Let them confuse the airheads who try breezing through the codes.

BUMPER STUMPERS

Some kids make bicycle name plates using coded sticker labels. The key to the code is the colon. If it is black, note the letter that comes **after** it. If it is green, rivet your eyes on the letter **before** the colon. Pay no heed to the color of the letters: they turn the fender enders into bumper stumpers.

TRY THE KEY: CRACK THE CODES

Who owns each bike?

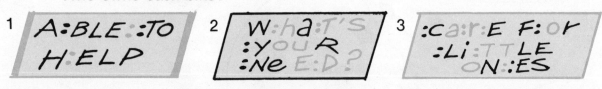

1 A:BLE :TO H:ELP

2 W:ha:T'S :YOUR :Ne E:D?

3 :ca:r:E F:or :Li:TTLE ON::ES

STEW CLUES

What's cookin'? To ladle up the answer, blend together — in the order they come — each of the following as you read the lines in a recipe:

— A **black** lowercase letter in print.
— An uppercase letter in script.

You'll find that each line contains a word, while colors and numerals set nosy nerds sniffin' and whiffin' in other directions.

TRY THE KEY: CRACK THE CODES

1

• WASh a TOMAto
• ADD 4 raW sh*a*llots
• tURN on *H*eat:350°
• *S*et in coPPEr KeG.

2

3 RIpe LEeks
2 ciNNamoNsTiCKs, DicEd
1 *H*ard Roll OF *W*heat
*T*urn on OVeN timeR.
LE*T* broil until BLACK.

SWITCH DITCHER

To ditch those with an itch to sniff out a secret, try this twist on a letter switch. If a word has two, three, or four letters, switch only the first two letters:

GO EAT A BEE'S WING

OG AET A EBE'S IWNG

If a word stretches five letters or farther, flip-flop the first two **and** the last two letters:

I PREFER HONEY MYSELF

I RPEFRE OHNYE YMSEFL

HINT: This key works best with words that have no more than six or seven letters. Also, the word strings can be made to look mighty mysterious with big, bold letters snipped from newspapers, magazines, and other products of printing machines.

TRY THE KEY: CRACK THE CODES

1 AWTHC HSISP NETRE AHRBRO.

2 ASLE NEDDE ALST RFIDYA.

3 RAE HTEY LAIESN RFOM LPUOT?

4 ARIN URINDE HTERI CSAYR CSHEEM.

5 RBUEC OSLD ESVNE ITCKEST LAREAYD.

6 IBKE VOER OTWADR HGOTS SILADN OTNIGTH.

Become a quote noter, a comma chaser, a semicolon eyeballer. That's how you can decipher secret sentences written with this key. If a word is followed by a comma (,), a semicolon (;), or wrapped in quotation marks (" "), read the word as part of the message. All other markings are brain bogglers, except for this: #. It signals the end of a secret sentence.

TRY THE KEY: CRACK THE CODES

code ~ o ~ gram ⬜⬜⬜⬜⬜⬜⬜⬜⬜

DEAR T4:

IF I, "WISH" MAYBE I, "COULD," JACK WILL = JOIN, YOU, BUT, NOT TIFF. HE ASKED "MY" →

COUSIN, JUDY. = HE "IS" HAVING, A GOOD TIME ← BUY A, PINATA; FOR THE "PARTY"#. AND

"I" WILL BRING CHIPS. = JACK HAS ALREADY; PROMISED, HER, "I" WOULD; NOT GO; TO, THE→ PARTY. "HER" HOUSE,# ↓ IS TOO FAR. "MAYBE" I WILL CALL "NEXT" MONDAY. ↑ WILL THAT TIME;# BE "OKAY"#?

B3

FLIP-FLOPPERS ON DOORKNOBS

As you read from left to right, take heed of letter pairs shown between these marks: ( )   [ ]   >< { } .

Tr (Pa) e {eZ}   [p] Rfor>em< R

In each case, flip-flop the letters. That is, switch them around to pin down the meaning. And don't let size or color trip you along the way:

TraPeZe   peRformeR
TRAPEZE   PERFORMER

HINT: For a room full of laughs, make doorknob hang-ons. Place a riddle under each knob-hole cutout, and run its coded answer top to bottom or corner to corner.

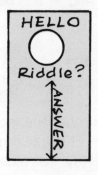

TRY THE KEY: CRACK THE CODES

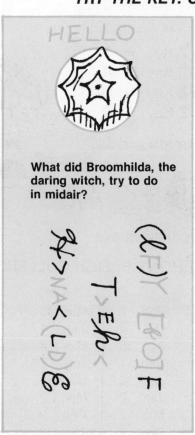

What did Broomhilda, the daring witch, try to do in midair?

When people exchange Valentines, how do they talk?

How did Busybody, the unicorn, get hurt?

1   2   3

HAZY DAZE

To wend your way through a hazy-dazy message, use both the Calendar and A-to-Z Keys:

CALENDAR KEY

Jan. = 1	Feb. = 2	Mar. = 3	Apr. = 4	May = 5	June = 6
July = 7	Aug. = 8	Sept. = 9	Oct. = 10	Nov. = 11	Dec. = 12

A-TO-Z KEY

POSITION:	1	2	3	4	5	6	7	8	9	10	11	12	13	14	15	16	17	18	19	20	21	22	23	24	25	26
LETTER:	A	B	C	D	E	F	G	H	I	J	K	L	M	N	O	P	Q	R	S	T	U	V	W	X	Y	Z

Take the number the month represents and add it to the day. Then let the sum of the two numbers cue the placement of the letter in the A-to-Z Key. For example:

MONTH   DAY

Mar.	3 = (3 + 3)	=	6th letter in A-to-Z Key =	**F**
Dec.	6 = (12 + 6)	=	18th letter in A-to-Z Key =	**R**
Feb.	13 = (2 + 13)	=	15th letter in A-to-Z Key =	**O**
May	2 = (5 + 2)	=	7th letter in A-to-Z Key =	**G**

HINT: To signal the letter A, use any combination of month and day that totals more than 26.

TRY THE KEY: CRACK THE CODES

Each hazy daze gives a two-word daffynition for the phrase above it. The two words are divided by the line.

THE TIDES
1   =

Dec.	3	July	6
Feb.	1	Mar.	12
Jan.	4	Sept.	11
Aug.	20	May	4
Apr.	10	Nov.	4
		Jan.	13

BLACK PEPPER
2   =

Dec.	7	May	15
Aug.	6	Jan.	4
Feb.	3	July	23
Mar.	2	Jan.	18
Nov.	15	Feb.	3
Apr.	1	Oct.	8
June	12		

PHONY SLEIGH PULLERS
3   =

Feb.	7	Mar.	15
Oct.	4	Jan.	4
Apr.	15	May	4
Aug.	1	July	7
Jan.	13	Mar.	1
Jan.	2	Mar.	2
Mar.	2	Feb.	3
Dec.	6	June	12
Feb.	3		

22

ARABS AND ROMANS

Arabic numerals combined with Roman numerals can also mystify a prying eye.

ARABIC NUMERALS: 1   2   3   4   5   6   7   8   9   10

ROMAN NUMERALS: I   II   III   IV   V   VI   VII   VIII   IX   X

Messages are written like those in Hazy Daze, except a mixture of Roman numerals is used in place of months and days. By seeing how **TENT** was "pitched" below, you'll discover how the key works:

XX	= (10 + 10)	= 20th letter in A-to-Z Key =	**T**
I2II	= (1 + 2 + 2)	= 5th letter in A-to-Z Key =	**E**
3V6	= (3 + 5 + 6)	= 14th letter in A-to-Z Key =	**N**
64X	= (6 + 4 + 10)	= 20th letter in A-to-Z Key =	**T**

With pen and pinking shears  , you can make stamps that look like these. Be careful, however, to leave the proper spacing around the Roman numeral **I** so that a friendly code cracker can note such differences as these:

IV = 4   I V = 1 + 5   IX = 9   I X = 1 + 10

TRY THE KEY: CRACK THE CODES

Starting from the top, what does each stamp say?

1.
X5 IV
II1
6X2
1
V3V

2.
X2III
10VI
2I2
3IV7

3.
24II
VI69
304
6XIII

4.
II O IV
1371
V2II
95
9X1

5.
202
V
3X5
II
3XX2

6.
XV2
18XII
IX
XV83

23

BOOKSTACKS

When Jan stacked the books below and left the note at the side, it was easy for Chris to crack the code. Can you?

Each numeral in black tells you which book to count down to. The arrow shows the direction in which you should read the letters in the title. And the green numeral that follows the arrow tells you how many letters to count in that direction, until you come to the coded letter.

For example, the key to the first letter in Jan's coded message is 8← 7.

8 means **count down to the eighth book.**
← means **read the title from right to left.**
7 means **count into the seventh letter from the right (T).**

The ■ separates one letter from another, and the ▲ signals the end of a word. Now it's your turn to go on and...

TRY THE KEY: CRACK THE CODES

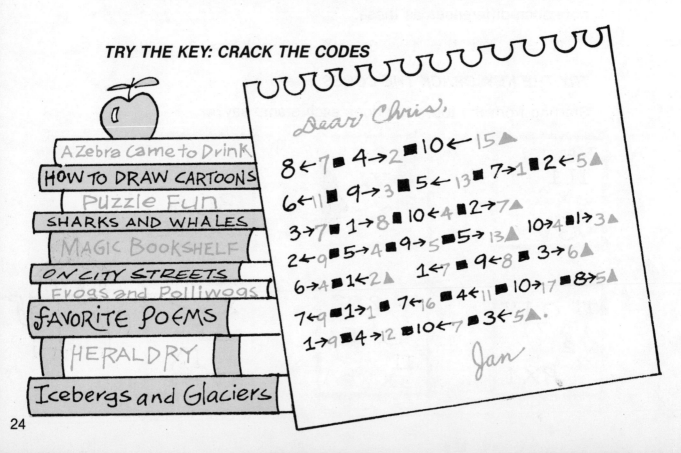

THE PLACE-NAME GAME

Like Bookstacks—with a count-down, count-in way of attack—the Place-Name Game aims to muzzle and puzzle a code prober. To see how it works, picture the place names at the left as if they were letters in a grid.

34123242-
ELKO
LUND   =
CARP
DYER
4122233143

34 12 32 42 —

E	L	K	O
L	U	N	D
C	A	R	P
D	Y	E	R

4 1 2 2 2 3 3 1 4 3

Then look at the first pair of numerals at the top of the grid (**34**) and think of it as a two-digit numeral. The first digit tells you how many rows to count down (**3**), and the second digit tells you how many columns to count in from the left (**4**) to find the secret letter: **P.** The next two-digit numeral (**12**) means: count down one (**1**) row and in two (**2**) columns. There you will find the next hidden letter: **L.**

Now that you know the pattern, what message do the other number pairs — including those below the place names — spell?

TRY THE KEY: CRACK THE CODES

HINT: A dash (—) separates one word from another. Colors and types of letters are misleads — detours to a dead end!

11322545-

1

D	A	Y	T	O	N
E	L	M	O	R	E
H	A	M	L	E	R
G	O	S	H	E	N

14 314523

53245 36-

2

K	o	h	a	l	a
N	U	M	i	l	a
W	A	i	h	e	e
P	a	h	a	l	a
N	i	n	o	l	e

41 35 124125 36

46 — 313616 —

3

K	i	n	G	S	t	o	n
L	E	a	s	b	U	R	G
G	U	i	l	f	o	r	d
S	T	E	R	L	i	n	g

41126 47 12238

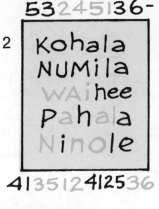

CLOCKFACES

In Code 1 below, place a ruler on the **long** hand of the first clock and let your eyes run along the edge of the ruler in the same direction as the hand points. What letter does the ruler cross, or run through? That letter (**S**) is the first in the coded message.

Now place the ruler on the **short** hand of the first clock and see that it points to the letter **I**. Keep going in this fashion — from long hand to short hand, clock to clock — and you'll be able to tell the hidden meaning in a matter of minutes! And note each time (no pun intended) that a green letter signals the end of a word.

TRY THE KEY: CRACK THE CODES

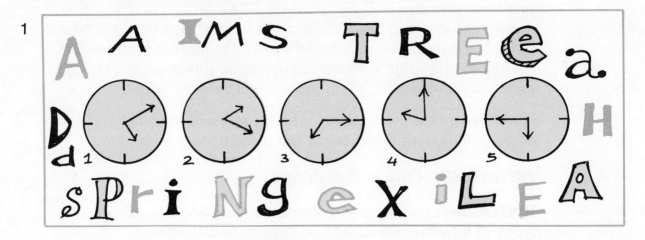

ASSIGNMENT: CHALK TALK

The Befuddler Muddlers disguise their messages as chalkboard assignments in the classrooms of Central Junior Spy School. To figure out their chalk talk, switch the letters divided by an asterisk:

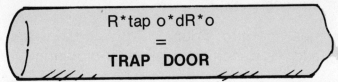

R*tap o*dR*o
=
TRAP DOOR

Pay no attention to size and color. They keep "Sneaky Petes" away from this frisky letter play.

TRY THE KEY: CRACK THE CODES

TONIGHT'S HOMEWORK

MATH   PP. 146-53

1 R*OCHR*AD HD*IO*EUT

2 DEO*CA*RE*T Y*GMNS*AIM*U

3 a*RiE*sd y*EEBO*rw i*GE*VS I*sga*NL

4 H*TE*RE yr*AS*d By*En*OD Pm*Uk*PN*i A*PC*th

READING

1 U*tn*R dOR*O N*KB*O i*Egt*h Tm*i S*e

2 Hl*Ei Cp*O*R*e A*ld*nig*N

3 h*SOP i*p NG - ML*AL s*eCAA*l O*tr

4 a*Se*tLi*LTe i*DH*S BH*eN*id A*grae*G

SCIENCE

1 O*hlia*dY O*Bat PaA*Re*d

2 t*sc*ok Prt*EE*zl si*tcs*K, p*a L*pl*e, N*aD e*JLy*l o*dUGN*hT*us

27

DIAL THE FINAL FOUR

To create something that looks like a dispatch from a Siberian spy, do this:

1. Write your message: **HELP IS ON THE WAY**

2. Break the message into groups of four letters each and, if necessary, add X's to complete the final grouping.

   HELP ISON THEW AYXX

3. Using a four-digit key — such as 2341, 4132, or some other arrangement of the numbers one through four — decide how you want to reorder the letters in each foursome to bury the message. Also, poke a dot under the last letter in each word.

HELP	ISON	THEW	AYXX		HELP	ISON	THEW	AYXX
2341	2341	2341	2341	OR	4132	4132	4132	4132
PHEL	**NISO**	**WTHE**	**XAYX**		**EPLH**	**SNOI**	**HWET**	**YXXA**

TRY THE KEY: CRACK THE CODES

HINT: In each case the message-sender cued the key to the code in the last four digits of a telephone number. For example, in the first telephone number, the four-digit key **1423** means that, to unscramble the coded letters in **KEPE**, note the following:

The first letter is in position   1: **K**
The second letter is in position 4: **E**
The third letter is in position   2: **E**
The fourth letter is in position 3: **P**

The dot under the P also signals the end of a word. What other four words remain?

1	762-1423	KEPE ATIS FUPF PRLE IXXP
2	559-4312	ACLP ADLE RAED INAG WITS MIDN XXLL
3	614-3124	AIRN DAYY ILWL ASWH WAAY OOFT RIPN SXTX

BLABBER JABBER

Codemates with computers enjoy toying with unique features of their machines. Instead of typing a sentence like this:

FIX THE LIGHTHOUSE BEACON

. . .they might:

1. Break it up or combine letters in all sorts of strange places:

   F IXT HELI GHT HOU SEBEA CON

2. Boldface, or heavy-print, the beginning and ending of each word:

   F IXT **HE**LI GHT HOU **SE**BEA **CON**

3. Pepper the page with periods and these marks: >< .

   F. IXT **HE**LI   GHT. HOU   **SE**BEA. CON

And, as you can see, the results look like the blabber jabber of Martians off their orbit.

TRY THE KEY: CRACK THE CODES

1 **D. ID**YOUS >< MEL. **LB.** A >< CO **N.**

2 LEA >< VE. BEF. >< OR E. M >< E

3 P.U >< TPE. N >< CI. **L. S** >< TU. **BA**BO. VE >< LE. F >< **TE. AR**

4 **D. ON** >< OT. TELLA**N** Y >< ON**EA** BOU. **T** TH >< **E**HO - L.L. OW**BE** >< A. **M**

5 **W. E**RO. DE**TH** >< E. **R**A. >< PI. DS **O.** >< **N** SN. AK. **ER**I.VE >< **R**

6 **A.** RE**Y.** OU >< RE. AD Y**FO** >< **R T.** H. EBL >< A. STO. - F >< **F?** T >< H. **E**COU. NTD >< O. WN. I >< **S.O.** >< **N.**

ANSWER FILE

DOTS 'N BLOTS, *page 4*
1 AWESOME
2 HANG GLIDING
3 BLABBER PUSS
4 GRASSHOPPER PIE
5 CREAKY STAIRWAY
6 ELECTRIC GUITAR
7 WHEELCHAIR ACE
8 PUPPET SHOW

TELESCOPES, *page 5*
1 CASTLES IN THE SKY
2 QUEEN OF HEARTS
3 PAINT YOURSELF RAINBOWS

BRANDING IRONS, *page 5*
1 FLOAT THE RAFT
2 ROPE OFF THE AREA
3 PEANUTS

FIZZLER CURLS, *page 6*
1 FORTUNE COOKIE HOLDS
NEW CLUE
2 COMPUTER SOFTWARE
3 ELEPHANTS MARCHING TRUNK
TO TRUNK
4 DINNERS FOR DINOSAURS
5 TO GET AT THE LUCKY PENNY,
BREAK SEAL

FLAG TAG, *page 7*
1 WATT?
2 SOLO (SO LOW)
3 CHOPSTICKS
4 WATERPROOF
5 WALNUTS

SPAGHETTI LETTERS, *page 8*
1 INSIDE MAILBOX
2 JERRY HAS MEASLES
3 HUCKLEBERRY GLEN

VOWEL SHAPES, *page 9*
1 PURE CINNAMON
2 SPOOKY NIGHTMARE
3 NEAR FURNITURE STORE
4 NOISY LOUDSPEAKER
5 SNOWFLAKES AND ICICLES

NUMBER/LESS PLATES, *page 10*
1 BOULDER
2 CIDER (BESIDE HER)
3 BOOMERANG
4 DRAWBRIDGE
5 SANDWICH
6 DRAGONFLIES

CODE-A-CARDS AND BOOKMARKS, *page 11*
1 DON'T BLOW IT. ENJOY!
2 SIGN UP FOR MY PARTY
3 WAVES OF GOODBYE
4 **TO:** POLAR BEAR; **FROM:** GRAY SQUIRREL
5 ALL'S WELL THAT ENDS WELL

BUBBLE DOUBLES, *page 12*
1 BEACH UMBRELLA
2 I AM ON YOUR SIDE
3 WILL YOU TRADE THAT COIN?
4 PUSH THE BLUE BUTTON
5 MESSAGE IS ON FLOPPY DISC

AUTOGRAPHS & STICK-UPS, *page 13*
1 HOT TIP
2 POPCORN
3 RED INK

FRAC FLACK, *page 14*
TODD: JACK LUTZ GAVE ME A COMPUTER
GAME.
BOB: WHAT IS IT ABOUT?
TODD: RACING BUGGIES OVER MOON
CRATERS.
BOB: BET I CAN BEAT YOU.